Nothing you don't already know

Nothing you don't already know

Remarkable reminders about meaning, purpose and self-realization.

Book & cover design by Manon Binkhorst

Photo by Steven Borghouts

Editing by Julia Willard

ISBN: 978-1718704329

www.alexanderdenheijer.com

alexander@purposologist.com

"Life is a school where you learn how to remember what your soul already knows."

– Unknown

INTRODUCTION

In September 2015 I started an Instagram page called @Purposologist. I wanted to have a platform where I could share ideas about self-realization and purpose. All my life I've been fascinated with these topics, and in 2015 I felt the desire to share some insights that I thought might be useful to others.

Self-realization means two things to me. On the one hand it's about the actualization of our potential; to become what we are capable of being. On the other hand, it's about getting to know our true selves. This book is about both.

The words I share on Instagram have been read and shared by millions of people. I'm very grateful for all the support and feedback that I have received so far. The encouragement and support of so many people resulted in the idea to write this book.

I once read that if you write to yourself, you write to an eternal audience. That's exactly what I did. What I have written was initially meant to make sense of myself, and to remind myself of the things that I believe are important in life.

Each page in this book has a new insight for you to reflect on. The book is laid out in such a way that allows you, the reader, to read it from start to finish or to flip it open to a page and use that insight as a daily reflection. The chapters of the book represent my own journey. They follow a path that may be recognizable to many of us; from being stuck in a place where we don't want to be, to being in a position where we can inspire others.

I have also been inspired by many people on my journey; philosophers, psychologists, spiritual teachers and many more. In the back of the book you'll find a list of people that have inspired me in one way or another.

This book is not meant to tell you what to do; it's only meant to make you think. It's not meant to tell you the truth either; it's meant to encourage you to explore the truth for yourself. Just see what resonates with you. I believe the best books don't necessarily teach you anything new, they just point to that which is already inside of you.

The only thing that I can do is share with you what I have learned, and hope that it will inspire you. The word 'inspire' literally means 'to breathe life into'. That's the most beautiful thing words have ever done for me and I hope the words in this book may do the same for you.

Alexander

CONTENTS

1.

A CALL
FOR CHANGE

You often feel tired, not because you've done too much, but because you've done too little of what sparks a light in you.

Many of us spend our working days running from desk to desk, solving urgent but insignificant problems. Our managers are constantly searching for ways to get more out of us. We're habitually living in the future, thinking about the next quota to make, the next meeting, the next car to buy, the weekend. We're constantly trying to get somewhere instead of being where we are. We miss the only moment we ever have access to. **The Now.**

We spend more time at work than with our loved ones. And when we come home, we are busier connecting to our devices than to the people we love. We have become little more than zombies. Yet we wonder, 'Why am I so tired?' We figure it's because we work too much.

What if we're not doing too much, but rather we're just doing too little of what truly matters?

**It's not hard work that exhausts us most,
it's meaningless work that exhausts us most.**

The most harmful road is not the road with the toughest obstacles, but the road that's heading in the wrong direction.

Sometimes life pushes us in such a way, whether it be through circumstances or our own choices, that we end up walking down the wrong road. We may not have wanted this but somehow we ended up in this situation. And with each step this road is leading us further away from our true North.

Turning off a familiar road is one of the most difficult things to do. We may be afraid of the unknown.
Maybe we're afraid that all the other roads are even worse. What if we never find a better road?

Fear holds us back from choosing another road. And so we continue, one heavy foot in front of the other, hoping that one day things will end up resolving themselves. But in our hearts we suffer.

Unless we have the courage to get off the road, we will only get farther away from our true North. We may not know our destination yet, but our heart will tell us when we're headed in the right direction.

The reason many people suffer is not that life is too tough; it's that they haven't found something worth living for.

Life consists of suffering. There's no getting around it. A fulfilling life is not a life that's without suffering, a fulfilling life is a life that's worth the suffering.

Many of us struggle to find meaning in life. We are so absorbed by our work and our daily distractions that we do not take time to reflect and ask ourselves where we would like to go in our lives. Many people are not even aware of what they are aiming at. And because of that, life slowly becomes aimless and unfulfilling.

You may be perfectly aware of what it is that you are working **on**, but are you also aware of what you are working **for**?

What is your aim? And to what extent is what you are currently doing aligned with that aim? There's a lot of fulfillment to be found in aligning yourself with a meaningful aim, and to work toward it, every single day.

Hardship without purpose may weaken us.

Hardship with purpose may strengthen us.

If we have something to aim for, then the unavoidable struggle will have a sense of meaning to it. Hardship stretches us and enables us to realize our potential. This is how we grow. We don't grow without pressure. But if we are unable to find meaning in hardship; we just wither.

It depends a lot on the story we tell ourselves. Do we see hardship as a meaningless way to make us suffer, or do we see it as a meaningful way to make us stronger?

Sometimes, if people discover something valuable beyond themselves, and they dedicate their best energies to it, they transcend their own suffering. As Friedrich Nietzsche said,

'He who has a why to live for can bear almost any how.'

You can't discover your passion by thinking about it.

How many of us have said, "I think about it all the time but I can't figure out what my passion is"? Well the reason we can't figure it out is that it doesn't work that way. One does not discover passion by thinking about it. We don't **think** passion, we **experience** passion.

Passion comes as a by-product of putting effort into something meaningful. The only way to experience passion is to put effort into that which is important to us

Passion manifests as a result of wholehearted effort.

Go follow your interests. Experiment, explore, discover. Do things worth doing until you ignite that spark inside yourself. But remember, igniting your spark is like falling in love. That's the easy part. Staying in love and weathering the inevitable storms is the hard part.

It takes time, commitment, and continuous effort to keep a fire burning. The more care and effort you put into it; the better it gets.

When a flower doesn't bloom you fix the environment in which it grows, not the flower.

Just as a flower needs certain conditions to blossom, so do human beings need a certain environment to flourish.

We are much more influenced by our environment than we think. The friends we hang out with, the culture we are a part of, the families we grow up in, and even our social media feeds. What we are being exposed to everyday influences our thoughts, behaviors, and eventually our character.

Set up your environment in a way that's supportive of your growth. Try to get rid of useless distractions. Surround yourself with good people. Keep your house in order. Stretch yourself by putting yourself in new situations. Don't let yourself get too comfortable.

We can alter our environment to a certain extent, but it takes courage to leave an unhealthy environment, and it takes wisdom to understand what kind of environment is best for our health. Sometimes the best way to change ourselves is to change our environment.

Never underestimate the importance of having a place where you can show up as you are; where your whole self is welcome, not just a part of yourself.

You have no idea how many of us are constantly trying to live up to an image that other people may find important. This is quite exhausting because it costs a lot of energy to constantly regulate yourself. There's a constant fear of doing something that doesn't correspond with the image. The problem with fear is that it suppresses creativity, joy, curiosity, and spontaneity.

There's a saying in Zen that says, 'Tension is who you think you should be. Relaxation is who you are.' The less we have to worry about fitting in, the more we are able to stand out. Not to be better than others, but merely as a result of becoming who we truly are.

It's vital to find ourselves a place where we can be who we are, a place where we feel at home. If you don't have such a place, go look for it. If you can't find it, create it.

2.

LEAVE THE
ORDINARY

Changing is not the problem; letting go of your resistance to change is.

When we resist inevitable change, we may become frustrated. Frustration is often the result of trying to resist change. In fact, it's the result of resisting life itself. It's our resistance to the flow of life that disrupts our progress. We believe change is difficult, but it isn't change that's so difficult.

Think about it, many of the seemingly difficult things in life are actually quite easy. Quitting a job, ending an unhealthy relationship, asking someone for a date... it only takes one decision. How easy! What is hard though is to make that decision. It's the hesitation to make a decision that consumes our energy, not the decision itself.

Once we have made the firm decision to change, there is no way back. Making a decision is about closing other options. When there is no option left, we have focus. Once we have let go of our hesitation to do something, we can focus all of our energy on doing it.

It's not the mountain in front of us that we must overcome; it's the hurdle within ourselves.

Every time a decision is made,

a path emerges.

When we make a decision, a new path emerges. If nothing emerges, you haven't made a decision; you've just come to a conclusion. A conclusion says 'you should do this' whereas a decision says 'Ok let's go.' Our rational mind is good at generating conclusions, but our emotional mind makes decisions. Reason is our navigator but emotion presses the gas pedal.

The word "decide" literally means "to cut off". It's about cutting off all other options; chopping away what's irrelevant. A firm decision is like a future set in stone. That's why visionaries are so powerful; they see a future as if it already exists, and they decide to make it happen. Think about Steve Jobs who said, "We started out to get a computer in the hands of everyday people, and we succeeded beyond our wildest dreams."

So the point is, start with the vision in mind. Make it crystal clear where you want to go, or who you want to be, and ask yourself if you're willing to take responsibility for it. Decisions and responsibility go hand in hand. Without responsibility there can be no decision. So find out what it is you want, and cut off everything else that's irrelevant.

Believe in yourself.
You become what you
believe you can be.

Henry Ford once said, 'Whether you believe you can do a thing or not, you are right.' To be able to get something done, we must believe it is possible, even when no one else does. We must have faith in ourselves. We have to trust that we will find a way, even if we don't yet know the way.

Most people judge their ability to achieve something by looking at their current skills. We don't have to master every skill right now. If our goals require more of us than our current skills, we may have to work on our skills instead of just lowering our aim.

People will say to you "you can't do it", but what they are really saying is "I would be too afraid to try that, myself." Don't let others with limited views affect yours. If you believe beyond a doubt that you are able to do the thing you are about to, then you are already half way there.

Getting to know a diverse group of people leads to a better understanding of yourself.

If we hang out with people from all over the world and from all walks of life, we'll find it helps us get to know ourselves better. Have you ever considered the fact that you wouldn't have a sense of identity if you had never met someone else? You are only an extravert compared to an introvert.

Meeting people from different backgrounds and cultures can teach us some valuable lessons. One is that we can learn more from people who disagree with us than from those who agree with us. Another lesson is that people may have varying beliefs, ideas, looks and behaviors, but despite our differences, when you look closely we are much more alike than we are different.

So go out and meet people. Travel. See the world that exists outside your community. It's enlightening, not just because of the places we see, but because of the people we meet. And it's not just about the people we meet and the stories we share; it's about getting to know ourselves in a different way as we are seen through the eyes of others.

You've been waiting
for a moment that
may never happen.
The realization that
this moment may
never happen, is
the moment you've
been waiting for.

We're all searching for answers. We travel the world in search of ourselves. We read books. We go to seminars and workshops. We listen to teachers and gurus. We are in desperate search of the ultimate answer, thinking that one day we will find it and all of our problems will be solved.

We think that one day, we will be saved. One day, our talents will be discovered and we can live our dream. One day, true love will find its way to us. One day the search will be over, and we will be free. All these thoughts have one thing in common; they assume that our desired future will one day just show up in the present.

What if you would realize that the future you dream of might never find its way to you? Would you stop waiting for it, and start creating it?

Don't spend your entire life building a ship without ever tasting the salt of the ocean.

Some people spend their lives trying to create the perfect conditions to live, without really living.

Too many of us believe happiness is a future event. And before we arrive, we need more money first, have a successful career, find a partner, settle down. And only then we will arrive at the destination of happiness. But when we arrive, we will realize happiness isn't there.

Happiness is not found at the finish line. There isn't even a finish line. Life is not a race to be finished; it's a dance to be danced. And only if we allow ourselves to enjoy the dance, can we let happiness in.

One day your life will flash before your eyes and you don't want to see a slide show of all the things that turned out to be irrelevant in your life. Life is happening right now. We've got one shot. Taste the thrill of life. Have the full experience.

The point of living isn't to arrive at the future; it's to arise in the present.

3.

OVERCOME
FEAR

The fear of making a mistake is more harmful than the mistake itself.

To live our lives trying to avoid mistakes is one of the biggest mistakes we can make. Inspiring people make many mistakes. They take initiatives. They experiment. They do things they've never done before, and they sometimes fail.

Failure is a crucial part of life. It's okay to make mistakes as long as we learn from them. Inspiring people recognize their mistakes, admit them, fix them, and learn from them.

They aim for excellence, not perfection. They accomplish, not because they don't fail but because they keep on trying. Ultimately, it's not the mistakes that matter; it's our ability to learn from them that really matters.

One of the most powerful things someone can do is to ask for help.

Sometimes we need a little help and sometimes we need a lot, especially if our dreams require more than our own effort. For many of us, one of the hardest things to say is 'Please help me.' It's a sentence that makes us feel vulnerable. It requires us to admit that we can't do everything alone.

Growth oriented people are the first ones to ask for help when they need it. They don't judge themselves for asking help and they don't judge others for needing help. They just know that no one can realize their dreams on their own.

Think about this: when we help someone we get a feeling of fulfillment. Doing things for others without expecting something in return makes us feel good about ourselves.

So next time you need help, allow someone else that chance to feel good for having helped you. In return, you may feel good about yourself, too.

The future is only scary
for those who are unable
to deal with the present.

Our fear for the future is directly linked to our willingness and ability to deal with the present. Everything we don't face today, we postpone to the future. This is how our thoughts about the future become terrifying.

Whatever we postpone, we some day have to face. And even worse, by putting things off, they grow in size. If we learn to deal with whatever life throws at us in the present moment, we build a sense of confidence and power. Every obstacle we overcome gives us more confidence. And the more confident we become, the more we can deal with.

Now is always the right time to deal with life. Face it. Look life straight in the eye and just know that there may be things that you don't want to face, but there is nothing that you cannot face.

We increase suffering
by trying to run
from it.

We release suffering by learning to live with it.

Most of our suffering is produced by the fact that we try to run away from it. There's a saying that goes, 'The best way out is always through.' If we want to live without fear, or any other emotion, we must first learn to live with it.

As Rumi said, "The cure for the pain is in the pain." In the end, people who are afraid of life are actually just afraid to experience their own pain and emotions. If we open ourselves up to experiencing all possible emotions, we open up to life. Instead of trying to get rid of unpleasant feelings, it's more rewarding to learn to relax while experiencing an unpleasant feeling.

Welcome everything, no matter how unpleasant. The release of our suffering is found in the unconditional acceptance of it.

Stars don't shine because they want to be seen; they shine because they are stars.

One of our core needs is the need for recognition. As long as we don't feel recognized we experience some kind of fear that we are not enough. Social media owe a big part of their success to the human craving for validation, and it seems like we have forgotten what it means to have true confidence.

Confidence is not about looking strong and invulnerable. Confidence is about being who you truly are with all your imperfections because you are not so concerned about what others think of you; you are more concerned about what you think of yourself.

The insecure compete against other people, while the confident compete against themselves.

Being confident doesn't mean we have to show everyone how good we are; it means that we know we are enough without having the need to show off.

Dive deep into your fear.
Face it. Embrace it.
Make friends with it.
This doesn't mean
you will no longer
have fear; it means
fear will no longer
have you.

Whenever we have to do something that we are afraid to do, we must remember that the most courageous people are not those who are never afraid, but those who are not afraid of feeling afraid.

We must learn to feel the fear without letting it hold us back. Fear is just a sensation in our body. We can feel it, but we should not become it. We **are** not afraid. We **feel** afraid. Just let it come when it comes, and let it go when it goes.

If we can train ourselves to feel the sensation of fear without trying to get rid of it, we will be able to overcome it. Just witness your fear, allow it, and release it. See it as a friend that gives you useful signals, but never make it your master.

Without change there would be no challenges.

Without challenges
there would be no
evolution.

Without evolution
there would be no
life.

It has been said that change is the only constant in life. Most people fear change because change brings challenges and challenges bring discomfort. People don't like discomfort, because they are attached to the way things are.

Comfort has never stimulated someone to grow and evolve. Comfort is addictive. It leads to laziness and inaction. It slowly dulls the spirit. It makes us stop growing. And if we stop growing, we start dying.

Change may bring challenges, but with every challenge comes an opportunity to grow and evolve.

Whenever change finds its way into your life, do you worry about the things that you may lose, or do you look forward to all the possibilities that it may bring?

Fear may motivate
but only love inspires.

Our fears are born out of unfulfilled needs, such as the need for safety, the need for love and the need for recognition. Fear is driven by self-interest.

Fearful people are afraid that they don't **have** enough or that they **are** not enough. Fear always needs something. Fear always wants to get. That doesn't mean fear is bad, it's just a survival mechanism that reveals an unfulfilled need.

Once we learn to fulfill these needs and we let go of fear we make room for love, and love is not interested in taking because it doesn't need anything. Love is appreciation, and appreciation has no needs.

Love is not an emotion; it's a way of being. And once we raise our consciousness to a state of love by overcoming our fears, all we want is to connect, create and contribute. Love always wants to share.

You can do things better or worse than someone else, but you cannot be better or worse than someone else.

We may criticize what people **do**, but we cannot criticize what people **are**. Judgment exists only in the field of doing, not in the field of being.

It's important to distinguish the field of doing from the field of being, because it can positively transform the way we see ourselves and other people.

What we do is open for feedback. It can be measured, compared, and judged. But what we are simply is. We are not our behavior. What we are lies beyond judgment, measurements and rankings. Even beyond understanding.

That doesn't mean that we're equal either, because equal is also a judgment. What it does mean is that we are. You are who you are, I am who I am. Everyone is indescribable, and that which is indescribable is incomparable.

Opportunities unfold as a result of following one's inner compass.

Carl Jung said, "The pendulum of the mind alternates between sense and nonsense, not between right and wrong." Human beings have an internal compass that helps them navigate between what makes sense and what doesn't.

No one in the world can tell us what makes sense to us; we have to discover that ourselves. Other people can advise us, but they can't make the decision for us.

When we find the courage to do what makes the most sense to us, we will find opportunities at places where we didn't even look in the first place. New worlds will open up.

Listen to your internal compass and let it guide you. You will find that the more you listen to that inner voice, the more you'll be open to opportunities that come your way.

4.

KNOW
YOURSELF

The way you see yourself is reflected in how you treat yourself.

Whether it's the jobs we go after, or the partners we choose to share our lives with, we rarely chase what we want. Rather, we chase what we think we deserve. The beliefs we have about ourselves determine our ambition.

The way we see ourselves is reflected in the way we live our lives. It's reflected in the people we choose to be friends with, the organizations we choose to work for, the food we choose to eat, and the clothes we wear.

As a result, the world will see us in the same way as we see ourselves. We will receive feedback that strengthens the image we already have of ourselves, which becomes a loop.

But when we make the firm decision to raise our standards, and to live up to those standards, we will begin to change the way we see ourselves. And as a result, the way the world sees us will change too.

Your world is a mirror.

To see what you cannot see you must break through the beliefs that limit your view.

When we believe we already know something we stop exploring. Beliefs are like conclusions. These conclusions become the lenses through which we see the world. Our beliefs can be so strong that we actually see what we believe. To those with a fearful heart the world is a dangerous place. To those with a playful heart the world is a playground. We constantly see what we believe to be true.

If we filter our views through our beliefs, we don't actually see; we project. Projecting leads to judgment; true or false, right or wrong. This is not how we learn; this is only how we confirm what we already believe. To discover new truths, we must question our beliefs.

If we want to grow, we must learn to be completely open; to observe without judgment. True learning occurs when we arrive at the same place over and over again until we recognize it for the first time.

People who frustrate you may reflect a part of yourself that you haven't embraced yet.

When I was young I used to work in a denim shop and I often heard people say, "I hate mirrors". Of course people don't hate mirrors. They hate the reflection of a person they're unhappy with. To get rid of that unpleasant feeling it's easy to blame the mirror and avoid it.

But if we avoid the mirror, the problem is not really solved. Only the confrontation with the problem is solved. Unfortunately, this is how most people "solve" their problems. We eliminate the trigger – whether they are people or situations, instead of looking at ourselves. Other people do not always cause our unpleasant feelings; often they merely trigger unpleasant feelings that are already within us.

Blaming others for the way they make us feel is like blaming the mirror for the way it makes us feel. The key is not to blame the trigger, but to look in the mirror, and see what it is about ourselves that makes us feel so uncomfortable and then face it.

You cannot truly connect if you're putting on an act.

Much of the quality of our lives is determined by the way in which we feel connected to others. One of the most important skills to learn in life is how to connect to people and build meaningful relationships.

One of the keys to connection is authenticity. It's hard to connect to those who are putting on an act, hiding behind a mask.

Authenticity may be more important than personality. The word personality comes from the Latin word 'persona', which means mask. Most of us try different masks during our lives only until we become confident enough to let go of our need to wear a mask.

We are not our mask; we are the light that shines through.

When our light shines through, we express our authentic selves. When we express our authentic selves, we invite others to do the same. And only then, can we connect from the heart.

Go against the rules if you must, but never go against your conscience, even if the rules demand it.

Some people do anything for the sake of success, love, or recognition, even at the expense of their conscience. But everything we gain in life at the cost of our conscience is ultimately a loss. We can ignore our conscience, but we can't ignore the consequences. It violates our soul. Go with your conscience, because somehow it already knows what is right.

Do the things that make you feel good about yourself, not the things that make others feel good about you.

We shouldn't do the things that are right to look good to others, we should do them because it's the right thing to do. Stay true. At the end of the day, it's not so important what others think of you; it's more important what you think of the person you see in the mirror. The more you respect the person looking back at you, the more you are able to appreciate those around you.

What you call 'I' is like a brand.

It's nothing more than a concept.

Think about your favorite brand. Now ask yourself 'What is a brand exactly?' Is it the product that's being sold? No, the brand has a product, but it is not the product. Is it the building in which the employees work? No. Is it the employees? No, the employees work for the brand, but they are not the brand. Is it the logo? No, the logo refers to the brand, but it is not the brand. Then what is the brand? If we get to the core of what a brand is, we find it is only an imaginary concept. It's just a made up story.

Now think about what we call 'I'. What is I? Am I my body? No, I have a body, but I am not really the body. Am I my thoughts? No, there are just thoughts passing by, but they are not me.

Then what is me? In the end, what we call 'I' is just a concept. Just like your favorite brand. It's just a story.

"Who would you be without your story?"
– Byron Katie

There's a light that
shines within you.
All you have to do is
let it shine through.
Open the curtains.
Take off the mask that
hides the light and
light up the world.

If we ask people who they are, they usually start with their names, followed by what they do for a living. If you ask them to continue, they may tell you their background and preferences, and maybe even their values and beliefs. But none of that is who they are, it's their story. We are not our story.

As soon as we try to define ourselves, we reduce ourselves. If I would say 'I am a writer,' all of a sudden I have reduced myself to being a writer. I am not a writer; I am a human being that happens to write. At the core of what a human being is is being itself. That's indefinable.

All of our definitions, thoughts and stories are just curtains that block our inner light from shining through. Our task is to pull back the curtains.

If we are able to let go of everything that we are not, we may eventually realize what we are; we may suddenly re-member our true Self.

"The question 'Who am I?' is not really meant to get an answer; the question 'Who am I' is meant to dissolve the questioner."

- Ramana Maharshi

5.

TRANSFORMATION

It's not finding yourself
that's hard;

it's facing yourself that is.

We travel the world to find ourselves, but aren't we just running away from ourselves? Carl Jung once wrote, "One does not become enlightened by imagining figures of light, but by making the darkness conscious."

It's easy to look in the mirror and see our bright side. It's easy to acknowledge our talents and gifts. It's much harder to shine a light on the things we don't want to see. The failures, the jealousy, the fear, the hatred. Or the hurt little child, hiding deep within ourselves.

To see ourselves the way we are is one of the most difficult things to do. It requires radical honesty and courage. If we are able to look at our dark side without judgment, we may be able to accept ourselves as we are. If we no longer see our dark side as an enemy, we may befriend it. When we bring light to darkness, the darkness dissolves and our light will shine even brighter.

The courage of self-realization is letting go of all that is familiar yet false.

To realize ourselves, we must first learn to be our own authority. This means we must challenge the ideas that are thrown upon us by our family, culture and society. We must learn to live by our own inner authority. It takes immense courage to do this. It takes courage to see that we are being conditioned by our culture. It also takes courage to let go of ideas that are so familiar to us. Yet if we want to realize ourselves, then what is true must become more important than what is familiar.

If we seek to realize ourselves, we may sometimes have to isolate ourselves for a while. It's hard to get to know our inner voice if we're constantly influenced by the voices of others.

If we learn to listen to our inner voice and become our own authority, we can realize ourselves. And only then can we truly renew and enhance ourselves and the world around us.

Some people never attempt to escape from prison for the simple reason that they don't know they're in prison.

Sometimes a prison is so obvious that we don't even see it. Whether it's built by others or by ourselves, the prisons that confine us are not made from walls, they are made from thoughts.

We think we're free to do what we want, but our actions are limited by the thoughts we believe to be true. The thoughts we don't question become our limits.

When we realize that we are not our thoughts, only then can we escape the prison. In fact, the mind itself is the prison. We can escape by realizing that we are not our thoughts, we are not even the thinker. We are only the witness. Thoughts are just leaves floating in a river; we are not the leaves; we are the river.

We are not contained within the limits of our thinking; we are contained within the limitlessness of our being.

Sometimes in the midst of a breakdown you find the key that unlocks a breakthrough.

The greatest breakthroughs often arise from the deepest struggles. The most enlightening art is often made in the darkest of times. The dirtiest roads often lead to the most beautiful places.

Even entire organizations often need to experience a **breakdown** first before they have a **breakthrough**. Sometimes the light cannot be seen unless it's dark.

So whenever you go through hard times and you hit rock bottom, accept it. Don't fight it. Instead, use it as a foundation to build a better life. Never be a victim. Rock bottom is nothing more than a story we tell ourselves. Reframe the story and move on. Life is not about what happens to us; life is about how we bounce back.

The most beautiful lessons always hide under the dirt. Dig a little.

Your ego wants you to be the best *in* the world.

Your spirit wants you to be the best *for* the world.

Before we transcend the ego, we see ourselves as separate entities, disconnected from the whole. We think in terms of 'my' life, and 'your' life. Therefore, we focus on ourselves and we use the world and everything in it to enhance our lives.

After we have transcended the ego, we see ourselves as interconnected parts of the whole. We no longer have a life; we are life. Therefore, we focus on life as a whole and we use our individuality to enhance life in its broader sense.

This doesn't mean we conform ourselves, it means we integrate ourselves. To conform means to become of the same form as others, which reduces our individuality. To integrate means to use our individuality in a way that it adds something to the world.

Paradoxically, that is the dance of life, to increase our individuality while simultaneously increasing our connectedness with others.

The moment you discover your purpose is the moment you unlock your greatest source of energy.

If we keep doing what we've always done, we seem to forget why we do what we do. This is a habit. Many people live their entire lives out of habit.

We may eat healthy, we may exercise regularly, but without a sense of purpose we may not live fully. Without an exciting reason for waking up in the morning, we will never experience the amount of energy we have access to. Without strong intention, we become a slave to our habits.

Ask yourself, 'What is the difference I'm trying to make?'

The moment we discover our purpose is the moment we tap into an infinite source of energy. This is the moment we realize we weren't tired; we were just uninspired.

As Mark Twain said,
"The two most important days in your life are the day you are born and the day you find out why."

Life is meant to be lived by ourselves, but not just for ourselves.

Our basic needs such as safety, belonging, and recognition drive us until these needs are being fulfilled. The fear of not being able to pay our bills will keep driving our decisions until that fear disappears. The fear of not being recognized drives us to be seen by people.

Once these needs are being met or outgrown, our consciousness expands. We become aware of our true nature and we feel the desire to realize ourselves. As we grow, we'll soon find out how our unique gifts contribute to the needs of the world. And there it is: we find meaning and purpose. We realize that a life lived only for ourselves can't have much meaning. Our consciousness is now less concerned with our own interest, and more with the common good.

Beyond our fears and beyond our ego we realize that everything we've ever wanted is to make a positive difference in the world. We suddenly remember what our soul has always known: the ride of life is not just meant to be enjoyed; it is meant to be enhanced with our presence.

The world around you matters little to your well-being. What really matters is your relationship to the world around you.

In essence, the world itself is neutral to our well-being. It's the way we relate to the world and everything in it that determines our sense of well-being.

Many people think that social media make us depressed, or that money is the root of all evil. We also tend to think that some people make us happy, and others make us unhappy.

But in reality, it's the way we relate to things that matters. It's not social media that makes us depressed; it's our relationship to it. It's not money that makes us unhappy; it's our relationship to it. It's not our partner that makes us happy; it's our relationship to him or her. Instead of changing the world around us, it may be better to change the way we relate to the world.

Invest in your relationships. Start with the relationship you have with yourself, for that will reflect itself in all the other relationships you have.

The eternal tension between what is and what ought to be either causes frustration or transformation. The choice is yours.

There are two problems in life; either there is something we don't want, or we want something that isn't there. The first reason creates aversion. The second reason creates longing. Most of the time, both situations trigger frustration.

To let go of the frustration we must learn to accept reality as it is. Nothing is right or wrong in itself. See the world exactly as it is: perfectly imperfect.

Acceptance doesn't mean passivity. It just means we don't argue with reality; we don't resist the truth of what is. Once we have accepted that things are exactly as they are, we can now focus our attention on what we want to manifest in the world. It's interesting to see that transformation usually happens as a result of accepting something completely.

6.

MAKE
A DIFFERENCE

Sometimes the person who can see the most clearly is the one we call blind.

How often do people tell us to be more realistic? But what is that, "being realistic"? History books are full of people who were called unrealistic for thinking they could build an airplane or fly to the moon. Now we know who were really the unrealistic ones. Realistic is only a perspective, a point of view.

Sometimes the most realistic people are the ones we call unrealistic. We call them blind. They don't seem to see the obstacles on the path. They don't see reality.

"Obstacles are those frightful things you see when you take your eyes off your goal." – Henry Ford

Sometimes, there are those rare people who are not focused on what is; they are focused on their vision. They are able to see what is yet invisible to others. And that's the point, to not just see clearly what is, but rather to see clearly what is possible.

Be bold enough to
know that you can
make a difference.

Be humble enough
to know that you're
a limited creature.

To make a difference, we must be confident enough to think that we have something to offer. We are way more capable than we think, and it takes boldness to discover that. Without boldness, we may think that we have little to offer. So we barely try.

However, take boldness too far and it turns into arrogance. Take it even further and one becomes delusional. To prevent us from becoming delusional, we need humility. We need to understand that no matter how strong we are; we are not omnipotent. No matter how much we know; we can't know everything. We're flawed and finite creatures, and by admitting our vulnerabilities, we remain humble. If we don't admit our vulnerabilities, life may eventually humble us the hard way.

Know your power, but now your limits too. Keep moving. Remain on the narrow path, that's where you'll find excellence.

Satisfaction comes from being good *at* something.

Fulfillment comes from being good *for* something.

Mastery is the key to satisfaction. To master something means to enjoy it. It feels good to be good at something.

This may explain the joy of video games. The better we get, the more we enjoy it. Play is fun, and to be a good player is even more fun. Some people can play video games for days in a row. However, the question that usually arises after a while is, 'What use is playing video games all day?'

It's great to develop our talents and to become extremely good at something, but if we are unable to use our talents for something meaningful, we may not experience lasting fulfillment. We experience a sense of meaning when we do something that is beneficial to our own lives, but that sense of meaning becomes even greater when it's also beneficial to other people's lives.

The point is not just to be good **at** something, it's to be good **for** something.

Distraction leads to inaction. Don't let today's pleasure destroy tomorrow's treasure.

We live in a time of instant gratification. Our attention is being hijacked all the time, as we constantly check our smartphones and crave shots of dopamine wherever we can get it. We are modern day junkies, addicted to our screens.

Can you remember the last time you spent hours doing nothing without feeling the urge to do something? Aspire to be that person again. Switch off your phone more often, or even better, do a complete detox for a few days and see how it will change you for the better.

Develop patience. Learn to work on projects that bring you lasting fulfillment instead of instant gratification. You can start today by asking yourself the question,

'What is the most meaningful use of my time right now?'

You slow down your progress by rushing the process.

One of the most common ways we slow down our progress is by rushing the process. We want everything **right now**. We seem to have lost our self-discipline, but what we have really lost is our patience.

Grass doesn't grow faster by tugging on it. The best things in life don't manifest instantly. We seem to overestimate what we can do in a month and we underestimate what we can do in a few years. We are in love with the result, but not the work - not knowing that it's the work that brings us fulfillment, not the result.

Take your time. Plant seeds. Give things their chance to grow. Keep moving, but don't stress out. Sometimes the best way to arrive on time is to stop running.

The more you focus
on the results, the
slower the process.

The more you focus on the process, the faster the results.

We don't achieve results by focusing on the scoreboard. We achieve results by focusing on the right efforts.

For example, if we want to lose weight, we don't lose weight by constantly weighing ourselves, or by longing for the perfect body. We achieve results by consistently making improvements to our lifestyle.

If we only love the fruit, we may not be willing to take care of the tree, but if we love to take care of the tree, we will most definitely reap the fruit.

The results we want tomorrow are manifested by the rituals we implement today. Focus on the rituals. It's all about the process. Take care of the small steps, and the results will eventually come.

Fight against what you hate and you will perish. Fight for what you love and you will flourish.

When we are constantly fighting against something, we increase our focus on the problem. This way we give power to that which we hate. This leads to anger, frustration, and sometimes even illness and death.

When we fight for something, we increase our focus on the solution. This way we give power to that which we love. This leads to passion, creativity, and evolution. It makes us rise above ourselves.

Take Martin Luther King, Jr. for example. He didn't fight **against** a nightmare, he fought **for** the dream.

As the polymath Richard Buckminster Fuller said, "You never change things by fighting the existing reality. To change something, build a new model that makes the existing model obsolete."

The secret of being at peace with yourself is to always do what you know you must do.

We create our own state of mind through the things we do and the way we explain those things to ourselves. Fact is, if we always act with integrity, we will always be at peace with ourselves. It's simple to be at peace with ourselves, but it's not easy to be simple.

If we don't do what we know we must do, we disturb our peace of mind. If we do this often, we may harm our self-esteem. We all make mistakes and we all make excuses. This is part of being human. The key is to correct ourselves as fast as we can. It's not easy, but everyone can learn this.

It takes wisdom to know what we must do and it often takes courage and self-control to then do it. The only way to do this is to practice. The more we practice to act with integrity, the better we become. Integrity comes as a result of continuously acting in line with our true values.

Don't chase happiness or success. They come naturally when you start seizing opportunities to make a difference in people's lives.

If we want to enjoy happiness and success, we must first understand that they are not goals. They are merely by-products of something else.

If we directly pursue happiness and success, we are just chasing shadows. But if we commit ourselves to improving the quality of life for ourselves and others, we may enjoy happiness and success as a result.

Add value to everything you do and to everyone you encounter. Enrich the world with your presence. Judge your value by what you've added to the world, not by what you've taken from it. It's the impact you have, not your income, that makes a difference in the world.

The key to a rich life is to enrich people's lives.

Somewhere during the
pursuit of my dream
I became aware that it
was not just the dream
I was realizing;
it was myself.

The pursuit of our dreams is never easy. It's a road full of obstacles and full of people who are trying to convince us that we are heading in the wrong direction. And still, we continue because somewhere deep inside of us there's a little voice that whispers, "Keep going".

We will face setbacks, disappointments, doubts, and obstacles, and every time we overcome another obstacle we become stronger and more confident. The struggles that we decide to overcome develop our strength.

And somewhere along the road we come to realize that it's not just our dream we are realizing; it's also ourselves. What we have built has also built us.

Maybe it's not about the dream; maybe it's about who we become while we're chasing it.

Don't be afraid to fail at things that mean something. Be afraid to succeed at things that mean nothing.

What is success? What if we are winning at work, but we are losing at home? What if we have a great family life, but we're slowly losing our spark because we're too afraid to go after our dreams? What if we make lots of money, but we hate our job?

A good life is about having the right balance. It's about knowing what really matters in life and living up to that. Never give up everything for the sake of success.

The point is not to be **successful**. The point is to **be** successfully.

Find out what ignites your spark, and cultivate that fire. Set inspiring goals. Invest time in your family. Help a friend. Look after yourself. Create something that didn't exist before. Enjoy the ride. You'll find that happiness comes as a side-effect. And when you're genuinely happy, you will automatically inspire happiness in those around you.

Everything that happens in life invites you to expand your ability to love.

One of the most difficult practices in life is the practice of unconditional love. To love life, regardless of what happens, is extremely difficult.

The best teachers of unconditional love are people and situations that hurt us. The people who act mean, selfish, greedy, or just harsh, are the most difficult to deal with. It's easier to judge them than to accept them. But if we learn to see through people's harmful behavior, we can clearly see that they are the ones that are harmed.

Instead of blaming people for their behavior, it's much better to see if we can understand their hidden needs. True understanding eradicates blame.

See everything that happens as an invitation to expand your ability to love, and you will find that your potential to love has no limits.

7.

INSPIRE
OTHERS

Great people don't influence you to be like them; they inspire you to be yourself.

Too often we are trying to change people according to a picture we have in our mind. We want to change them in a way that it matches our preferences. Inspiring people don't do this. They don't shape us the way they want us to be. Instead, they encourage us to shape ourselves in a way that's best for us.

Whether they are teachers, mentors or parents, great people inspire others to become more of what they already are.

It's not on us to change people. People are not our possessions. People cannot realize themselves if they cannot express themselves. We may support other people and encourage them, but it's on them to find their own way.

You don't inspire people by revealing your super powers. You inspire people by helping them reveal their own super powers.

If we solve people's problems, we produce followers. If we encourage people to solve their own problems, we produce leaders.

When we constantly solve people's problems, they will eventually depend on us. It may be great for our ego to have people depend on us, but it doesn't really help those people. It's much better for people if they can depend on themselves

Many people are afraid that others learn to do things better than them. It's because many people are insecure about themselves. Truly confident people are the most inspiring. They recognize their own unique value, and therefore they easily recognize and praise the value in others. These people possess one of the greatest gifts; the ability to inspire others to find their own gift.

Some of you see limits
in others while others
see potential.
No matter what you see,
it may say more about you
than it says about them.

Inspiring people will never tell us we can't realize our potential. Only people who have given up on their own potential say that. People see reflected in others what exists in themselves.

Inspiring people don't see in others what they can't be; they see what they are capable of being. They look at things in terms of potential. They are convinced that all of us can grow if we put our minds to it. The truth is, if we decide to look for limits we'll see them everywhere. And if we decide to look for potential we'll see it everywhere, too. It's all merely a matter of focus.

Surround yourself with people who acknowledge the limitless nature of your potential. Those rare people who love to see you grow into the person you are capable of being. And don't just look for such people, be such a person. It will help you to inspire others and you will find that your attitude will attract precisely the people you were looking for.

The most joyful state of being is being of service.

Aristotle said, "Where your talents and the needs of the world cross, there lies your purpose."

When we find a way to use our unique gifts in a way that it serves the greater good, we may experience the most fulfilling act in the world; the act of service.

When we are in service to the collective, we lose our sense of self and we are completely in sync with the present moment. It's the state in which the dancer becomes one with the dance. This state of being can only come to us if we completely surrender to the work we are doing.

If we serve others solely out of obligation, it may drain us. But if we serve others out of love, it may vitalize us. If we expect something in return, we are not really serving. Serving is not pleasing. Pleasing is done with the intent to get something. True service is selfless. It's one of the highest gifts we can give to others, but also to ourselves.

Interesting people may be noticed, but interested people are the ones who are remembered.

Inspiring are the people who have never lost their childlike curiosity. It's refreshing to meet people who are genuinely curious and interested. It's even more refreshing to be such a person.

Train yourself to focus on other people. Take the time to listen to people. Be open to what people have to say. Being open to people means that you are willing to be influenced by what the other person has to say. Open up and listen fully. Pay attention. True connection requires your full presence.

If you are fully present, you inspire the other person to be present as well. Find opportunities to connect. Sometimes the best thing you can do to people is to really be with them.

There is no present more precious than your presence.

The heroes that inspire you are the ones that give you a glimpse of your own potential.

Michael Jackson once said, "The greatest education in the world is watching the masters at work." Watching our heroes perform their craft can be extremely inspiring.

It doesn't matter who these heroes are or what they do, but what matters is that they provide us with an example of excellence. Their presence has the power to awaken parts in us that have been dormant. They show us what we can be if we give it our best, every single day.

They make us dream bigger, aim higher, and push harder. And it's not even them; it's a part of ourselves that we can see through them. A hero is someone who embodies a set of universal virtues. The point is not to idolize the person, but to embody those same virtues.

Find yourself some role models, some people you look up to. People you can learn from. This is one of the fastest ways to unlock your potential.

It's not selfish to live according to your values;

it's selfish to demand that others live according to your values.

It's on us to decide to live our lives in a way that we think is best. It's not on us to demand that others live their lives according to our values. Before we try and demand anything from others, we must reflect deeply on our motivations.

Before we go out and try to change the world, we may have to ask ourselves why we want to change the world in the first place. So that we can be happy? Why does the world need to change to make us happy? What makes us think we know what's best for the world?

"Yesterday I was clever so I wanted to change the world. Today I am wise so I am changing myself." – Rumi

Be wise and focus on the way you live your own life, and let others be free to explore theirs. Make your life a work of art. Your own self-realization may be the best way to inspire the world.

Don't work to survive;
work to create something
that survives you.

Time is our most valuable possession. We cannot buy time. We cannot get back lost time. We cannot even decide how much time we have; we can only decide what to do with the time we are given. We are just a flash in time and it's up to every individual to decide how to make the best use of it.

A fulfilling way to spend our lives is to use it for something that will outlive it. It's amazing to be part of something bigger than ourselves, to create something that lives on long after we're gone.

Use your time to leave behind something that is timeless. Leave a legacy. Not for the sake of being remembered, but for the sake of leaving the world a bit better off as a result of your existence.

Champions don't
show up to get
everything they want;
they show up to give
everything they have.

To live a deeply fulfilling life, don't strive to get everything you want from life. Instead, give life everything you have. Getting what you want causes a sense of achievement which is satisfying, but giving everything you have causes a sense of fulfillment, which may be more enduring and inspiring.

And guess what... we cannot control how much we get from life, we can only control how much we give. Judge your day by what you've put into it, not by what you got out of it.

Give life everything you have and you can never fail, because failure is not about the absence of rewards and success. Failure is about the absence of wholehearted effort.

At the end of the day, the question is not, **'How much of what was out there did I get?'** But rather, **'How much of what was in me did I give?'**

PEOPLE WHO HAVE INSPIRED ME THROUGH THEIR WORK:

ALAN WATTS
CARL GUSTAV JUNG
ECKHART TOLLE
ERICH FROMM
JAN BOMMEREZ
JORDAN B. PETERSON
KEN WILBER
LAO TZU
MARJA DE VRIES
MEISTER ECKHART
RICHARD BARRETT
RUMI
SIMON SINEK
S.N. GOENKA
ULISSE DI CORPO
VIKTOR FRANKL

ABOUT THE AUTHOR

Alexander den Heijer is a Dutch speaker, writer, and corporate trainer living in Amsterdam. His workshops and talks about self-realization and purpose reach thousands of people from all over the world. He is frequently consulted by organizations to share his insights on self-realization, personal leadership, and transformation.

Alexander has always been fascinated by the question, 'What makes people flourish?' this question has sent him on an infinite quest to understand human beings, especially himself.

He draws inspiration from many disciplines, including physics, biology, philosophy, spirituality, and ancient wisdom. He believes no single discipline can answer the questions that are facing us. We must see ourselves from different perspectives to understand and develop ourselves.

To book Alexander as a speaker or trainer, please visit www.alexanderdenheijer.com

To read more of his insights, visit Instagram.com/purposologist.

Made in the USA
Middletown, DE
31 January 2020